ON BLACKNESS AND BELONGING

THE RECLAIM PROJECT

Edited by Nosa Charles-Novia and Ayo
Olubode

Chapter introductions and Design Notes
written by Nosa Charles-Novia

All illustrations and designs by Samantha
Quitua

'and so we write ourselves into being'

CONTENTS PAGE

SANKOFA

EDITOR'S NOTE

It seems only fitting to open this anthology with the question which shaped the purpose and aim of The Reclaim Project, the Black question: *What does the term black mean to you?*

To me, Black means very interesting things. Having grown up in Nigeria during my formative years, then living in Thamesmead when I moved to the UK, an area colloquially known as 'Little Lagos', black to me never meant being the anomaly. I was never the 'black sheep' or 'the black friend'. My relationship with my blackness is mostly shaped by my proximity to Nigerian culture and heritage rather than by the standards set by an external, non-black voice.

But not everyone's experience is like this. Through conversation with friends and family, I learnt more about other experiences of black. Some of my friends saw black as I did while others saw it more through the lens of otherhood and race, usually as a result of the context they grew up in. I learnt that, though I was black, I could never speak conclusively on the black experience. I learnt to ask the black question again and again to every black person I met and again to myself after I met them.

The Reclaim Project is grounded in asking this black question to ourselves and others. The collective was founded on internal conversations between the diverse body of black students in the University of Warwick which would ultimately culminate in a poetry anthology embalming and preserving our experiences.

We started this conversation on campus by conducting campus interviews, which we called 'street interviews' where we asked black students on campus what black meant to them. The responses were varied and interesting. Some connected strongly with their blackness and saw blackness as a powerful symbol which spreads joy. Others felt fractured from the universal lack experience portrayed in social media and believed personal factors such as ethnicity and cultural background heavily affected experience of blackness; i.e a Black British experience would be different to a Ghanaian or Jamaican experience of blackness. The street interviews once again reified the idea of a fractal experience of blackness and rekindled our interest in hearing about different experiences.

The black question is not only important to internal black conversations and black rediscovery, but to the perceptions non- black people hold about us. It involves the secret, unsaid perceptions held about black, the subconscious prejudices and the current confusion around blackness. Asking the black question is imperative to sustainable cultural progression as well as self-evaluation.

So, I ask it again: *What does the term black mean to you?*

This anthology is a collection of poems from writers of different backgrounds and experiences addressing the black question and what it means to them. The poems are divided into three key sections which chronicle the ideas of blackness and belonging through three key experiences of blackness: 'The Black Question', 'Of Fracture and Finding' and 'Sankofa'. In the following pages, you may find power, force, anger, violence. You may also find exhaustion, despondency, contradiction, confusion, irresolution. Any journey of self-discovery and questioning involves all of the above and more.

I tried many times to write this note in a way which summarised the discourses of black within this anthology. But

I couldn't. Because this anthology is an introduction not a conclusion. Blackness is still ever-present and existing – meaning we must all still address and ask ourselves the black question.

So, before reading this and after reading it, ask yourself this question; *What does the term black mean to you?*

~Nosa Charles-Novia, Creator of The Reclaim Project.

To God who gave the vision
To the wonderful team for all their hard work
To all the beautiful poets who made this possible.
To the IATL department for their support.

I have crossed an ocean

I have lost my tongue

from the root of the old

one

a new one has sprung

— Grace Nichols, 'I is a long memoried woman'.

Prelude: 'No happy poems'

Black

    Poems

Black

    Bones

Black boy find your way back home

Black body bags make bad black poems

Black

Smiles

Black bones

       break

Black bones

       Broken

Black homes

shake

When these black poems are spoken

~ Maureen

The Black Question

Chapter introduction:

During the late seventeenth century, The Woman Question arose in Europe due to disruptions to the social order which troubled traditional categories of womanhood. Now, in a period chronicling similar troubled categories, a period where blackness is marked by both excellence and the legacies of slavery and Western encroachment, The Black Question arises.

The poems in this section address the black question; What does it mean to be black in today's society? What does the Black experience look like now? How does society handle/tolerate blackness? How do black individuals deal with their own raced identity? These poems explore the contested concept of being black in today's society; a necessary feat- especially as blackness continues to exist in the liminal space between adoration, appropriation, and demonization.

—

'Not limitation but celebration; surplus and not lack

Remove all my pieces and still what is left

Is black.'

mOTHERland

They said this was the motherland,

"England is the place for me", they sang

Therefore, Britain is home...

But is it really home when they shout, "Go back home!"?

Now it's an identity crisis

But all the government cares about is the immigrant "crisis", and the Brexit "crisis"

Because now England knows how it feels to be out of place

Born here but doesn't really belong

As my skin sticks out like a sore thumb

London is okay

But outside, some places are numb

To diversity

So, I think I should be called a Londoner

Cos if I went up to Sunderland or Northumberland

It could be a different story

My origin could be questioned without words

White eyes pierce into my red heart

To see whether my passport shares the same hue

Belonging is the sort

Of feeling, dictated by my black skin

Despite the fact, that blood deep

We're all kin

It's no motherland

When all I dream of is another land

Where there is no racism or stereotypes

Where I am not policed

Or criminalized.

It's a reality that some do commit crime

But statistically, white boys are more violent

"You want some? I'll give it ya"

16

And they ain't bluffing when they shout "Rush him"

Naah, in fact crush him

Echoing the words of their forefather

~Dianne

kyle rittenhouse, you f***ing sk*t, i hope you rot in hell

"isn't it cool being Black?

being feisty and ghetto and grown?

cause don't all Black girls

have curves? and the guys have huge cocks, right?

and you've got rhythm to dance the house

down – and don't get me started on your hair!

don't you love it? your hair?

it's so fluffy, i just have to touch it, i didn't know it could grow

so long. is it real? all Black girls

wear wigs or have weaves, right?

honestly, i think it's better to be Black now. didn't you just have a dude in the white house?

and will smith is on like every dvd in my house

and idris elba is gonna be the next bond. i've grown

up seeing you everywhere – girl groups, girl

rappers, girl sportsmen. and right

at the corner of my road there's a shop dedicated to your hair.

i mean, you have a whole month just to celebrate your skin.

and, like, if you're Black,

you'll never get cancelled for how you do your hair

and sure, you might get shot in the street like a dog, outside
your own house,

still so young you never even get to look at a girl

or a boy, never get the chance to be grown,

but hey, at least now you have rights!

the right to be profiled, the right

to have your community, your language, your hair

be gentrified by people who think being Black

gets you affirmative actioned into being unhoused,

that being Black makes you a man or a woman because there are no girls

or boys in the ghetto – everyone's already grown.

and if you forget for a second that you've grown up

having your body debated on and your hair touched

by white girls who give themselves cancer to look Black –

like you – but then won't even come into your house

because who wants to catch ebola, right?

and if you forget, for just a second, about girls and boys like you –

your people

being sent to the slaughterhouse

for being born the wrong colour –

then isn't it cool being Black?"

~Raechel

Am I Broken?

Am I broken?

The question I ask myself

Am I broken?

The question you ask yourself

Am I broken?

A version of me

Who sees, the news and with a heavy heart feels pain, anger and sorrow

As I see black people whose lives have been constantly taken by the gun of a police officer, by the gavel of a judge, and by the racism that remains prevalent in our society

Am I broken?

I'm boiling with anger,

eyes red, fist clenche

Eyes get watery but the tears don't fall

And I try to keep it all, together

I try to contain this feeling, but this feeling contains me

I punch the wall; one time, two times, three times, four

Till my knuckles can't take it anymore

I lay in bed, shut my eyes, hoping for an escape

But the escape never comes, instead I'm caged in my thoughts

Daytime, head in my pillow, I scream

Night-time, head on my pillow, I dream

Not like Martin, more of Malcolm or in the middle

As I wonder how far we've come and how far we will come

Thinking by any means, by any means necessary

Then asking myself whether that is necessary

And till this day, it's beyond me

Day in, day out, a black person dies

Day in day out, the victim's family scream "why God why?"

Day in day out, countless families wishing they had

the chance to say goodbye

Day in day out, the pain burns and grows on the inside

Day in day out, wondering if the pain will never leave but in my heart forever reside

Day in day out, I've burned out

And I can't seem to get up

Am I broken?

The question I ask myself

Am I broken?

The question you ask yourself

Am I broken?

A version of me

 doesn't see the news and refuses to watch it

Because I know what to expect

 and I'm now desensitised to it all

What is this feeling?

Is this apathy?

Am I broken?

I put down my phone, I turn off the television

I'm losing the vision

I'm losing the rhythm, I once had,

but not the blues

I'm losing the passion that once engulfed me like a rabid flame

Which now makes it harder for me to even chant 'Say Her Name'

And worst of all, I'm losing hope

Our greatest ally

So shall I, reclaim it?

I don't know if I can

For if there is no hope, there'll never be a chance

There'll never be a chance for me to make the world a better place

There'll never be a chance for me to take a stand

There'll never be a chance for me to take a chance

I wish I could last longer, be stronger

I wish I didn't have to walk away

24

I wish I had the stamina to finish this race

In doing so, potentially help my race

But I'm so far from the finish line

Matter of fact, I feel like I'm stumbling backwards, and all my progress has declined

And I just wish I didn't have to ask myself

if now or later is the best time

to just breathe,

to just breath

Am I broken?

The question I ask myself

Am I broken?

The question you ask yourself

Am I broken?

~D.A. E

The Fact

"Ezra, mate, you're black from afar but far from black"

A statement made funnier by the fact it was said

by a boy with white skin

But I believed it.

"Black from afar but far from black"

For so long I felt uncomfortable in this skin

A lone black sheep in the flock

At the mercy of the words of wolves

Who fed me bitter lies

Oreo, bounty, choc-ice

Labels that snacked away at my self-
perception

Leaving me doubtful of who I really was

Growing up was like

Walking a tightrope

You want to be true to yourself

But the fear of standing out   makes you lose balance

And fall

You shed layers to assimilate,

 left with artificial skin

That glistens on the outside

But is soulless within

And I would still be struggling on that rope

Were it not for a family whose branches

made sure my feet were firmly planted on the ground

So that I could connect to my roots

*Omo ajanaku ki ya arara, omo ti Erin ba bi Erin lonjo**

Because the truth is

The apple does not fall from the tree, despite the elements it may face

I realised that my identity was determined by me

And all the accompanying incoherencies

Not what others expected me to be

So

"Black from afar but far from black"

I look back and I can say with my chest;

"That's far from fact"

~ Ezra

*You are no different to your ancestors (rough translation)

The Black Question

The pieces of me are infinite to my mind,

multitudinous as the months that pass in a blur

they define and dictate the things that were,

who I was and who I am to be.

But 'black' is not so easy,

'black' is not so clear that I could,

without the doubt of defamation, tell you

it's meaning

tell you with no fear of condemnation,

of being misunderstood,

the possibilities and shapes that black could take

these convoluted questions that migrate their way across my
mind

are the enigma as to why I feel confined

in black.

Like the flow of time without a watch to tell it,

my colour exists as an indication to who

and to what I am. Yet still it is true;

the watch can be mistaken for time –

at once I'm the paradigm

29

of blackness, (whatever that means)

every and all stereotypes are presumed

of me and

I'm pushed into this box of patterns and

forms that feel formless because

lest we forget we were never meant to forge our

own place but take the given, chase dreams written without
our consent

but is this oppression story our best attempt

at black?

Yesterday and tomorrow converge into a

timeless cycle in which today is all that remains,

and today asks today The Black Question.

The ever-asking question with no

answer, with no such hope of

a finale, but instead a

yawning crack rifts space, time and identity…

But we're still here.

We still hold onto the flavours of our mother tongues

where excellence was not coloured and we still

see our differences despite our shared tag and we still.

Are. Different. Not limitation but celebration, surplus and not lack;

remove all my pieces and still what is left

is black.

~Mine

~

Of Fracture and Finding.

Chapter introduction:

Almost nothing is linear in the black experience. Much of the lived black experience is formed from the repercussions of black fracture: the transatlantic slave-trade, colonisation, immigration and the reordering of black land and people by colonial forces.

Home is often a conflicted and fractured idea for the Black Diaspora. We have moved, one way or another, whether forced or voluntary (and please note that voluntary is usually forced) and in that process of moving, things have gone missing. Lineages and heritage have become increasingly untraceable, cultures and practices forgotten, phrases and languages slipping from our tongues and minds. Many of us live in fracture and know it, even if we can't put it into words. This section is named after the tension 'of fracture and finding' which many black individuals find ourselves in. It is dedicated to black fracture, fear, frustration, tears, but also the longing for a home we have never known – the 'finding' and the journey we slowly start to take towards *Dahomey*, our true settlement.

"Some of us are waltzing to award shows,

Others are running from war."

BLACK & BOUGIE: On Delusions of Unity

"Them that's got shall get

Them that's not shall lose

So the Bible said and it still is news"

— God Bless The Child, Billie Holiday a.k.a. Lady Day

The ruling doctrine proclaims,

When it isn't vying to slander and defame,

The pursuit of fame and riches

As the main aim, these days

For 'Black Salvation'

It is declared: Be like The Carters!

Gone are the days of…

Heroes and martyrs…

No more Claudia Jones,

No, you are sorely mistaken,

These are the days of keeping up with

The Joneses

The black bourgeoisie sip champagne,

Raise a tightly-clutched glass,

While somewhere, under a broken street

Lamp, or eerie underpass,

A fiend overdoses, his life slips
away

Caressed only by the concrete,

His black skin does not mark him

As one of the great overachievers of our age;

The class aspirants, or the born-bougie

Often on the front page,

It simply marks him as

Decaying, lifeless,

Waste, refuse,

His death

His only refuge.

Some of us are waltzing to award shows,

And others are running from war

So-called 'Black voices' often only seem to

Heighten the silence,

The rumbling of the black masses reduced

To the noise of passing traffic

In the urban sprawl

Condemned to dull decline —

Socially, financially,

while the machines

Take the jobs away,

and more get pushed away

From schools

Meanwhile, Black Africa grinds on

In the background,

In the crosshairs

Of drought

And storm

It's just a dark body, nothing more,

Nothing less, a convenient fiction,

A plot device for bestselling

authors

Coltrane's A Love Supreme,

Or just 'Supreme' dreams?

Fashion moguls couldn't give a damn about compassion,

When they say it's global they mean:

Faceless 'third world workers' make it cheap,

Then the 'self-made entrepreneur' lets prices peak

Off false hype,

That's the mission

That's the 'vision'

Of individual escape,

And that's just great,

The old question remains though

Why integrate into

A burning house?

Shuffle deck chairs on the Titanic,

Just to get a safer view

Of the coming collapse

Some of us are waltzing to award shows,

Others are running from war.

~Trace

'Pot calls the kettle black' or 'On Black Hypocrisy'

Don't they know how hot the heat is?

Like a child placing their hand over the stove

Why aren't they scared of messing with fire?

How easily we can hate whilst being hated?

Nowadays I think even burnt hands crave the heat

Because everybody wants to hold the lighter

As long as there are enough sticks and stones breaking other people's bones to start a campfire

So what good is your movement if your picket signs are being made from the same firewood?

Why fan the flames of hatred when you know what it means to burn?

When they eventually extinguish your light and you are reduced to a mere hashtag,

Whose tongue will speak your name and hold the ashes?

Which minority will turn their bodies into protests for you?

Whose shoulder will catch your mother's tears?

If not of those whom you've marginalised

The child who is not embraced by the village will ~~burn it down to feel its warmth~~ set fire to your movement and find solidarity amongst the ashes.

~Maureen

'And so the debate continues' or 'On The Black Tax'.

I heard that separating your productivity from your identity is
the key
And somewhere in that extraction process,
You learn what it takes to be free
I'm no dentist but sometimes finding balance
Feels like pulling teeth

To work and to live; to balance both and still feel sane
Week in, week out
I carry out this extraction yet
I'm the one left in pain

What's good enough?
Am I doing enough?
Surely this is enough?

Look around you. What makes you think this is enough?

I can't argue back
My points fall short and
My arguments crumble to pieces
This inner critic won't stop and
I'm struggling to remember what peace is

Besides, what even is "good enough"?
The ever-shifting nature of that phrase is
As wonderful as it is frustrating
So, tell me why after hours of work
I'm still questioning

I'm still contemplating:

What's good enough?
Am I doing enough?
Surely this is enough?

Look around you. What makes you think this is enough?

Once again, my points fall short and
My arguments are obsolete,
I look to the sky, and I ask God:
Why put me here if I can't take the heat?

For my grandma, faith is a source of hope
Through the harrowing events of her life
Her belief in God helped her cope.

Compared to what she has survived:
I could say that I'm drowning, but what do I know of rain?
I could say that the work is too hard, but have I truly earned
the right to complain?
If I said that I can't take this pressure, would it be anxiety or
arrogance that's poisoning my brain?

Truth be told, I feel like a fraud sometimes
I am more privileged than every generation of my family so
far
But how can I say I'm not taking that for granted
Whenever my performance is subpar?

If could I talk to the next few generations of my family,
I would clearly say:
There's no inaction that could ever take away from your
worth
You don't have to fight for it, everyday

So maybe, I should stop asking myself:
What's good enough?
Am I doing enough?

And remember that
my existence is testament to the fact that
I have always been enough.

It's alright if sometimes, my points fall short
Fair enough if my arguments are old news
This inner critic won't stop, but neither will I
And so, the debate continues

~Triumph

'Westernized'

Mother tongue says to Nigerian girl

"Do you not get tired of fishing for the English in conversations that do not concern you —

That turn into conversations speaking about you?"

Nigerian girl responds

in English

Mother tongue tastes the barbed wire on her breath

and sees the inside of her mouth as

A border line

~Maureen

Mother tongue

1:

I did not learn my mother's tongue.

As a child,

I heard tiny traces

of *vwe* and *kpo* as I played.

But I never grasped the meaning

of sounds I vaguely recognised.

2:

I try to speak my mother's tongue.

Biting my inner lip

I force out breath

And release the flesh

vwe vwe vwe

A slingshot of trial and error.

I cannot *vwe* like she can.

Learning is a traumatic act.

I taste blood on my lips.

3:

I cannot speak my mother tongue.

and I burn on the inside.

Because my heart can never be understood

in the context which made it.

It tries to speak,

but is stopped at the border

where my mouth mistranslates

the code.

Mother,

who am I

if not yours?

I'm an outsider,

Dark skin with a white tongue

A fraud

betraying my heart with each syllable

I am of you,

but not yours,

And so I'm forced to Stand outside

The safe circle of my sisters' laughter and joy,

I'm the white sheep.

But Mother,

Whose job was it to teach?

Why did you not *vwe* to me? Or *kpo* to me?

And now the village doesn't accept me

Shouldn't you tell them its your fault?

That you sat silent then and you sit silent now.

4:

Daughter

You keep trying to be who you already are

Whether you can vwe

Or whether you can kpo

You have my blessing.

5:

I still cannot speak my mother's tongue

and I've paused trying

Because I'm still hers.

By the golden hue of our skin

By the wide spread of our smile

By the singular beat of our heart. I am hers

Within her embrace, I find a new circle.

She is my village.

~Nosa

Mo fe soro si yi

Mo fe soro si yi

I want to talk to you

    in a language that expresses the culture of my thoughts

Bo si bi bai

                                      Come here

Masa ere

                                       Don't run

Lest you trip over -And fall in

to the waters crossed,

Into my Yoruba heritage

Be still, wait and watch

For out of the depths comes

Rich culinary flavours

intonation of pride and strength.

51

Naija no dey carry last, olorun ti bless wa

Our deep-rooted aquatic plant of faith

No tide could wash away

The waves only shape our intake

Floating across many shores,

Depositing branches of communities

Though still connected and centred

to the land rich in minerals

Like trees we bear fruit

Sweet green, white and green

Yet there is more weight in its seeds

Our rite of passage,

Our inheritance to pass down,

The will of those before us, bundled into flesh

Because what we fear more than death,

Is to become a distant memory;

a lost culture

where no child has flavoured their tongue

with the language of the land,

to be naija only in check boxes of diversity and

inclusion forms,

for our names to lose its savor and lack the spice of its
meaning,

nothing but fleeting words.

~ Ayo

Sankofa

Chapter Introduction

'Sankofa' is a growing literary movement among black writers, formed from the *twi* word meaning "to retrieve" or "to go back". It is looking at history in a new light. Like its back-facing adinkra symbol implies, Sankofa is about looking back to look forward and focuses on reflecting on black history in order to re-envision ourselves. Reimagination - fictional, magical and idealistic reimagination - is a key part of black literature and the literature of other minority groups. We get to imagine ourselves afresh; to create a true home for ourselves in the vistas of our minds and slowly work towards making that dream a reality.

We get to take back our image, skin, stories, and bodies for ourselves, away from the schemas and labels that have been added to it for so long. Sankofa complicates the Western idea of linearity and singularity, which understands time only as chronology, and so places everyone on an isolated, individual journey. Rather, drawing upon African traditions, Sankofa operates in non-linear time. Past, present, and future marry together in a utopia where our ancestors get to live with us in our dreams for the future. Sankofa is a wild man's dream and a black man's prayer. It is the culmination of a fracture we stop resisting and instead reimagine. Therefore, Sankofa is the ultimate symbol of reclamation.

———

'Maybe our ancestors have already been to space

And back enough times

that we can consider ourselves

Celestial beings'

Black Space

I'm imagining a black space
Within a black space.

Endless darkness infused with light, forming a nebula.
The Milky Way is closer to noir abyss.

This black space doesn't blot light out
But instead emits iridescence.
Our shine near-incessant,

And when one light flickers,
The congregation makes sure
the constellation never fades

Rising to the call of the future -
We've already passed stratospheric.

When I see my sisters rise like Maya,
Continuing to strive,

My brothers thriving rather than dying, I know this is more
than lyric.

This is our greatest fight ever,

We're all in the ring, "Ali, Bomaye[1]"!

This is Huey before the gunshot,

Panthers in the modern day.

Better yet, we're the panthers of the future.

Maybe our ancestors have already been to space

And back enough times that we can consider ourselves

Celestial beings,

Come close enough to the heavens,

Been at tangent with the ether.

Afro-futuristic? To me that's

Sci-fi, high flyers,

Might hop in my saucer,

Like 'Ye I'll touch the sky, uh,

The laws of man are not something we adhere to

Apollo spacecraft really looking like ancient African burial
temples,

Egyptian pyramids.

So, what is a black space

Within a black space?

It is the darkest Moon turning to Sun,

illuminating the whole landscape.

~*Nyasha*

1) "Ali, Bomaye!", the chant of the crowd during the
infamous Rumble in the Jungle fight in Zaire (modern
day Congo) between Muhammed Ali and George
Foreman, which translates to "Ali, Kill him!". Often
considered one of Ali's greatest fights.

Though hope is foolish, still I will dream

There's a world
One with no ultimatums
One that reminds us we are limitless

It treats refugees as friends
Politicians as mortals and
Celebrates humanity in all its fullness

Crested cranes soar over the water
That was once poisoned by indifference
The flock flies on as communities
March towards their own deliverance

And with a smile I can proclaim:
'Lake Victoria is now dry' and
Only Nnalubaale remains

The master's house is crumbling.
Looted artefacts are being returned and
The Bluest Eye watches
As Black Beauty is affirmed

I hear children speak creoles and pidgins
I've never known a sound so sweet
I, too long for the day when this
Long Song is complete

The forests are being restored and
When kids go to school, their creativity's not
stifled
It's not watered down
It's adored

There are statues in my vicinity
Of women who have redefined solidarity
Standing together like birds of a feather,
United in the face of adversity

This world, this new world,
Has no place for greed nor those who excuse it.
Yes, there are still cracks and fractures
But it is my world and I choose it

Let dreaming be a fool's errand.
Because the wise are leading us to our doom and
Despite their many tries to
salt the earth, with their lies
the flowers of revolution are in bloom.

~Triumph Arach

Unapologetic

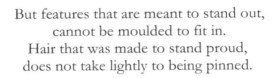

I have black features.
Hair that I wanted straightened,
nose that I wanted petite,
lips that needed squashing,
and eyes that I'd always squint.

But features that are meant to stand out,
cannot be moulded to fit in.
Hair that was made to stand proud,
does not take lightly to being pinned.

There is beauty in black features,
our stubborn strands tell us so.
Like DNA, it coils and writes
And so we must learn to let our beauty show.

~ Anju

Coloured

Coloured sand in

Coloured fields where

Coloured children play

In the middle, a circle of hair bobbles

and rainbow dresses stand and watch

two girls clap in synchrony,

There are smiles on their faces

as coloured fingers hit back and forth against each other

 in an intense game of Tinko.

A long while later, claps continue to sound.

The smiles have faded but their faces, still coloured

with innocent determination.

Suddenly,

one of the contender's hand slips

and does not match the next clap

She is out.

Her mistake making the other competitor

Queen of Tinko.

And from the crowd someone comes forward, to replace her

But as she walks back,

Coloured hands meet her halfway

and pull her into the Circle,

choruses and cheers, including the Queens' voice,

remind her of her great performance.

She smiles colourfully at them,

because she was never discouraged

and squats down to practice her claps

against the brown sand

These are girls of circle and clap and colour.

Who do not determine their hue by wins and losses

Or ups and downs.

Sometimes,

when life drains life

and the world is only black and white,

I see their coloured hands meet me halfway

in cheer and chorus.

All is well within this circle.

~ *Nosa*

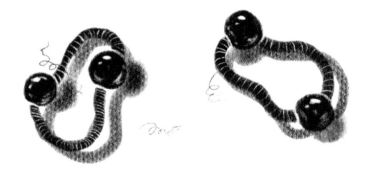

Pain is the currency

I'm known by my colour

Not colours

Certainly not true colours

A shade they threw at my shade

Never in control of the story this skin tells

The scroll that tells of humanities abominations,

Like a weighted vest this culmination of tissues

brings pre-installed issues -

cracked files

we were stolen and misused

Stripped of pride in melanated code

Returned with error messages, in red and bold

So we Lost love for our own

made to feel uncomfortable in our own

skin

They ridiculed our black and the things dipped in they called
sin,

 but appropriated the art it was influencing -

Sometimes,

I see pain in the shade of your hue

Alluring deep tones that whisper stories of survival

but other times,

when your hair defies physics and is rich in oils,

it tells a love story through
scent - and tells a journey
towards care

and acceptance.

At times, I catch the playfulness of mother tongues on the
lips of school kids

A sign of well-nourished roots, which grow

into well-rooted fruits —

free to dance with the wind but anchored to their mothers
stem

Today,

the aroma the wind carries is heavy with spices and heat.

Flavours sealed in Tupperware are carried in work bags with pride

You'd never imagine we'd become the story where pain turned into currency,

our Ancestors, the rich aunties who paid it forward

The bedrock

of our art

Written back into being.

We are the scars in time.

The answer to the history we are taught.

~ *Ayo*

'Questions'

A piece made to be spoken

Is it pain, is it joy? Is it shame, is it noise? is it rage, is it poise? is it build or destroy? is it brotherhood, sisterhood, fatherhood, motherhood/ killing one of our one cos he said he's from another hood? is it, restitution, or destitution, are we still slaves to our fate or are we blessed to choose it/ Is it broken homes, that make hopeless men, or is it the chosen thrones that give hope again/ Is it my crown or my downfall/ is it lost or have i found all the reasons we're dying or we're thriving/ It's hated and debated, evaded till emulated/ it's feared until they rate it, dismissed until they take it/ Is it, hall parties? Aff or it's yardie, speak the queen's english, or "you feel me, ya kna mean"/ Generational disconnect, is it disrespect/ Or do you disagree with us, coz this is next/ Is it celebrating difference in culture and religion, or is it finding unity in the empires that we live in/ Is it repentance or revenge, do i owe you a hand/ or is it each to their own coz they owned us like land/ Is it the poison that we're dying from? Is it our own doing/ Are we products of the past, the places that we grew in/ Is freedom a lost cause, we lose then we lost more/ We lust for a lot more, do you trust in God's law/ Is it faith in the fact there's higher powers to trust in/ Or is distrust and skepticism of what the rest may trust in/ Is it patience or rush in, stagnant or adjusting/ Is it british, american, or African/ Is it lost to time or am I mapping it?/ It's everything and nothing, so many things and one thing/ It's all I know, but it's all unknown/ Black ain't got an answer, we define the answers/ And that stays the same from here to the life after/ Black is my heart, my soul, my reason, even if I ain't got the answers this evening/ Black is the reason why I'd die and why I'm breathing/ But above all else, it's just something to believe in .

~ *Christopher 'Ceebo' Chivungo.*

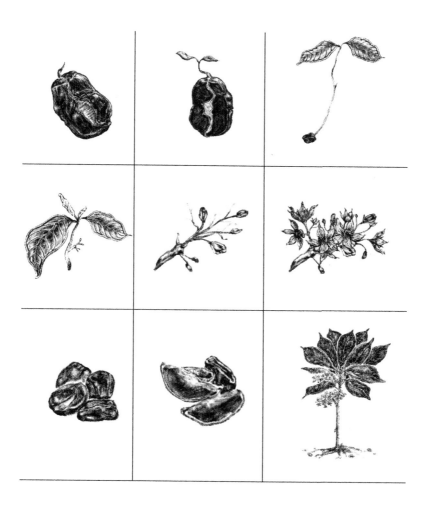

DESIGN NOTES

'I am a black ocean, leaping and wide,

Welling and swelling I bear in the tide.'

Maya Angelou

All images and designs in this anthology, including the front and back cover designs, were hand drawn by the amazingly talented Samantha Quitua. We worked closely with Sam to consider what designs would fit with the idea of reclamation, fracture and belonging and thought it would be worth explaining some of the inspirations behind ideas.

 The front cover image was inspired by Michelangelo's 'The Creation of Adam' painting which features two hands, God's and Adam's, reaching for each other. We chose to recreate the image with black hands, as. we felt that this reaching not only held the idea of longing to belong but the gap between the two hands embodies the tension of black fracture which hinders that belonging and embrace. This atemporal sea and sky location which the front cover is situated in, is a motif in other paintings within the anthology and promotion.

The painting of the black man and woman in this atemporal ocean was inspired by the biblical Adam and Eve but also heavily drew on the potent symbolism of water in black history and fiction. Water, particularly the ocean, in a lot of black poetry, has come to symbolise the distance and fracture caused by slavery and colonisation and the hope of meeting again. In Olive Senior's 'Hurricane Story 1951', water becomes a symbol of reconciliation between a mother in the UK and her son in the Caribbean, who closes the distance between the two by walking into the ocean. In Maya Angelou's poem 'Still I rise', she references the oceans tide as a mirror to the powerful expansiveness within black empowerment. In Grace Nichol's poetry, the ocean finds use as a symbol to emphasise distance and the reincarnation of the black woman persona who is 'a long memoried woman'.

The ocean imagery in this anthology is also inspired by the history of the Igbo landing where enslaved Igbo individuals took control of their slave ships and walked back into the ocean, choosing to drown themselves over being taken captive in a new land. Water, in black history and fiction, is a multifaceted imagery, evoking the idea of fracture, distance but also finding and a longing for home and belonging, which directly matches the themes explored in this novel.

Perhaps the most ambiguous design is the footnote drawings which are interspersed throughout the anthology. This design chronicles the progression of the kola nut plant. The Kola nut holds potent ceremonial symbolism in many West African ceremonies. It is broken and given as a symbol of hospitality, friendship and respect at weddings and ceremonies across West African cultures. We chose to include this image in anthologies as a visual way to trace themes of belonging and acceptance into a community.

As the kola nut is both seed and fruit, we thought there was something striking about the image of a seed/fruit growing into a tree which bore a harvest of fruit, seeds and flowers, which are featured on the front cover. The kola nut then, not only stands as a theme of belonging but becomes a visual symbol to mark the blurred, non-linear asynchronous time that holds importance in Sankofa and other African traditions.

To reiterate, this section was meant to provide clarity to the inspiration behind our images but all images remain open to interpretation.

So, after reading our anthology, we ask you again:

What does black mean to you?

~Nosa and Sam and Ayo.

ABOUT THE AUTHORS.

Profile page

Name or stage name: Dianne

Subject of study: Sociology with specialism in Race and Global Politics

Ethnicity and Nationality: Black British

Favourite Quote: "Not everything that is faced can be changed but nothing can be changed until it is faced" ~ James Baldwin

Contact details:

Personal Instagram: dxanne_d

Blog Instagram: merakiperceptions_

Profile page

Name or stage name: Ezra Olaoya, ETP (Stage name)

Subject of study: Politics Philosophy Economics (PPE)

Ethnicity and Nationality: Nigerian (Yoruba)

Favourite Quote: Even after the darkest night, the sun still rises (Victor Hugo)

Profile page

Name or stage name: D.A.E

Subject of study: PAIS

Ethnicity and Nationality: Black and Nigerian

Favourite Quote: "Our deepest fear is not that we are inadequate. Our deepest fear is that we are powerful beyond measure. It is our light, not our darkness, that most frightens us. Your playing small does not serve the world. There is nothing enlightened about shrinking so that other people won't feel insecure around you. We are all meant to shine as children do. It's not just in some of us; it is in everyone. And as we let our own lights shine, we unconsciously give other people permission to do the same. As we are liberated from our own fear, our presence automatically liberates others." ~ Marianne Williamson

Contact details: Instagram: d.a.e_x

Profile page

Name or stage name: Maureen Onwunali

Subject of study: Politics and Sociology

Ethnicity and Nationality: Nigerian and Irish

Favourite Quote: "until you bring what's unconscious into consciousness, it will control your life and you'll call it fate" – Jung

Contact details:
Instagram: @monwunali_poetry

Profile page

Name or stage name: Mine Oweh (MW)

Subject of study: Philosophy, Politics and Economics (PPE)

Ethnicity and Nationality: Nigerian and British

Favourite Quote:

"The only thing that is constant is change" - Heraclitus

Contact details:
Instagram: @heyaitsmw
Tik Tok: @heyitsmw

Profile page

Name or stage name: Triumph Arach

Subject of study: French and Linguistics

Ethnicity and Nationality: Black British (Ugandan)

Favourite Quote: 'You can't be hesitant about who you are' – Viola Davis

Contact details:
Email: trarach29@gmail.com
LinkedIn: Triumph Arach

Arach

Profile page

Name or stage name: Trace Asafo

Subject of study: Philosophy

Ethnicity and Nationality: Black, South Sudanese

Favourite Quote: "Reality is that which, when I think about it, does not go away." - Phillip K. Dick

Contact details:
Instagram: @ghettotekz

TRACE

Profile page

Name or stage name: Anju

Subject of study: Psychology with Education Studies

Ethnicity and Nationality: Black British/Nigerian

Favorite Quote: "If not now, then when? If not you, then who?"

Contact details:

Instagram: rochll.x

LinkedIn: Rowchell G

Profile page

Name or stage name: Ayooluwa Olubode

Subject of study: Economics

Ethnicity and Nationality: British- African

Favourite Quote: Psalms 23:4

Contact details:

Instagram: @thelightbox_1

Profile page

Name or stage name: Nosakhare Oghenetega Charles-Novia (Nosa Charles-Novia)

Subject of study: Film and Literature

Ethnicity/ Nationality: Nigerian (Benin and Urhobo), British

Favourite Quote: "Your life isn't small but you're been living it in a small way – Open up! Live expansively."

- 2 Corinthians 6:13 (MSG)

Contact details:

Instagram: @__isitbyforce

Work Instagram: @thereclaimproject21

Profile page

Name or stage name: Nyasha Kunorubwe

Subject of study: Law

Ethnicity and Nationality: Zimbabwean, Malawian & British

Favourite Quote:
"You can jail a revolutionary, but you can't jail the revolution" - Huey Newton.

Contact details:

Personal Instagram: Nyasha_kuno
Creative Instagram: fr33.souls

Profile page

Name or stage name: Ceebo/Christopher Chivungo

Subject of study: Politics and Sociology

Ethnicity and Nationality: Angolan and English

Favorite Quote: "I'm not a prophet. My job is making windows where there were once walls." ~ Michel Foucault

Contact details:

Instagram: ceebosw

Twitter: Cee_Artist Snap: crebosw

Ceebo

ABOUT THE MOVEMENT

The Reclaim Project is a collective of black creatives based in University of Warwick at the time of this anthology's publication. The Project is centered around promoting honest and open conversation and exploration of blackness between black individuals of different backgrounds, which we believe, in turn will lead to sustainable cultural progression.

Follow the movement on Instagram:
@thereclaimproject21

Printed in Great Britain
by Amazon